What the
Bible
Says About

Heaven

What the
Bible
Says About

Heaven

Encouraging Insights and Inspiration

Ed Strauss

BARBOUR
PUBLISHING

Published by Barbour Publishing, Inc., P.O. Box 719, Uhrichsville, Ohio 44683, www.barbourbooks.com

Our mission is to publish and distribute inspirational products offering exceptional value and biblical encouragement to the masses.

 Member of the
Evangelical Christian
Publishers Association

Printed in the United States of America.

CONTENTS

INTRODUCTION
THE HOPE OF HEAVEN

Since time immemorial, men and women have hoped for life after death in a place where they are joyously reunited with departed loved ones. They have longed for a place where the hardships, tears, and toils of this life are replaced by endless peace and bliss. They have dreamed of a place where bodies that were sick are made whole, a world where justice reigns and where broken hearts are mended. They have longed for *heaven*.

The Bible tells us that such a place exists—a place where all is peace and perfection, where all tears are wiped away, where we will finally understand the questions and problems that have burdened us, and where we will be consoled for the grief we have endured. The apostle John sums it up in the following words:

> *God shall wipe away all tears from their*
> *eyes; and there shall be no more death,*
> *neither sorrow, nor crying, neither shall*

> *there be any more pain: for the former*
> *things are passed away.*
> REVELATION 21:4 KJV

Maybe you have lost a loved one and wish to know what heaven is like. Or perhaps you're becoming painfully aware of your own mortality, and seek to know more about your eternal destination. Even if you're in the prime of a healthy life, you may want to be assured of heaven's certainty, to live on earth with a more eternal perspective. Most important, we all need to be certain that we're saved and going to heaven.

In society today, there are several persistent stereotypes and inaccurate descriptions of heaven—to the point that even many Christians have little idea of what to expect in the hereafter. So how can we know what is the truth and what is misconception? The Bible says, "Forever, O LORD, Your word is settled in heaven" (Psalm 119:89 NKJV). God's Word is also settled in what it says *about* heaven.

1.

OUR FUTURE HEAVENLY HOME

EARTH'S SORROW AND TOIL

For God's children, life is often a happy, satisfying experience. We have nice homes, good jobs, obedient children, trusted friends—sometimes almost more than hearts can desire. At times, it seems that all our prayers are answered, that we and our loved ones are kept safe from accidents, financial setbacks, and other misfortunes. And if we're in the throes of romantic love? Well, it hardly seems things could get better. We exclaim, "All this and heaven, too!"

If you're experiencing such a time, enjoy it while it lasts. For, as millions of believers can testify, you will also experience your share of hardship, trouble, sorrow, and injustice in this world.

You may, in fact, be going through a time when it seems that *few* of your prayers are answered, that you and your loved ones are *not* spared from accidents, financial setbacks, and other misfortunes. Life doesn't seem fair, especially when you see unbelievers prospering while you struggle to get by.

The truth is, God's people are not always successful, healthy, or trouble-free. Nor do they have everything their hearts could wish for. Rather, they know very well what the apostles Paul and Barnabas meant when they said,

> *"We must go through many hardships to*
> *enter the kingdom of God."*
> ACTS 14:22 NIV

The hope of heaven, therefore, has breathed life into many a discouraged believer.

Heaven is that land that may truly be called the land of the living. This earth is the land of the dying. There is nothing like the believing hope of eternal life to keep us from fainting under all the calamities of this present time.
MATTHEW HENRY

Still, we wonder why we face so many problems, setbacks, and troubles. *Why,* we think, *if God loves us, doesn't He bless us more on earth? Why doesn't He make our lives a little easier?* Many men and women of God have wrestled with such questions, and the answer often is, "We simply don't know." But we *do* know that things will be made right in heaven.

Your head may be crowned with thorny troubles now, but it shall wear a starry crown before long; your hand may be filled with cares—it shall sweep the strings of the harp of heaven soon. Your garments

> *may be soiled with dust now; they shall be*
> *white in a short time. Wait a little longer.*
> CHARLES SPURGEON

Often, when we're faced with illnesses, accidents, and bereavement, we wonder, "Where was God when this happened? Didn't we pray that He would protect us? So why didn't He?" Many of our questions won't be answered this side of eternity.

> *We may be robbed of our joys on earth*
> *by a thousand accidents, but heavenly*
> *joys are everlasting.*
> MATTHEW HENRY

In the meantime, Jesus has not promised ease in following Him. Nor has He promised that He will protect us from every problem.

> *Often here I'm sad and weary,*
> *As the days go by;*
> *Oft the scenes are dark and dreary,*
> *Teardrops dim my eye;*
> *But when this short life is o'er,*

We shall weep and sigh no more,
But rejoice forevermore
In our home on high.

"ANTICIPATION" BY
CHARLES W. NAYLOR, 1911

WE'LL UNDERSTAND ONE DAY

Many believers, after suffering grief and misfortune, want to talk to God and ask why He permitted such bad things. Abraham asked the Lord directly, "Shall not the Judge of all the earth do right?" (Genesis 18:25 KJV). There are times when it seems that God, the judge of all the earth, is *not* doing what is right. . .and we wonder why. Things make no sense. One day, however, He will answer our questions. We will understand one day.

Trials dark on every hand, and we cannot
understand,
All the ways that God could lead us to that
blessed promised land,

*But He guides us with His eye, and we'll
  follow till we die,
For we'll understand it by and by.*

*Temptations, hidden snares often take us
  unawares,
And our hearts are made to bleed for a
  thoughtless word or deed,
And we wonder why the test when we try
  to do our best,
But we'll understand it by and by.*

REFRAIN
*By and by, when the morning comes,
When the saints of God are gathered
  home,
We'll tell the story how we've overcome,
For we'll understand it better by and by.*

"WE'LL UNDERSTAND IT BY AND BY"
BY CHARLES A. TINDLEY, 1905

WE GO TO HEAVEN WHEN WE DIE

When we die, we are indeed "gathered home" as Charles Tindley says. Our bodies go into the grave and turn to dust—but our imperishable spirits go into the presence of God. The apostle Paul wrote:

> *For to me, living means living for Christ,*
> *and dying is even better. . . . I'm torn between*
> *two desires: I long to go and be with Christ,*
> *which would be far better for me.*
> PHILIPPIANS 1:21, 23 NLT

For believers, there's no stopover in some celestial way station (or purgatory). When we die and leave our bodies behind, we're almost immediately "present with the Lord."

> *So we are always confident, knowing*
> *that while we are at home in the body*
> *we are absent from the Lord. . . .*
> *We are confident, yes, well pleased*
> *rather to be absent from the body*
> *and to be present with the Lord.*
> 2 CORINTHIANS 5:6, 8 NKJV

ANGELS WILL CARRY US HOME

Some believe that when our spirits are freed from our mortal bodies, we will fly like the angels. Very likely this is so. But we don't know the path to heaven. That's why God sends His angels to take us there.

> *"And he will send out his angels with the mighty blast of a trumpet, and they will gather his chosen ones from all over the world."*
> MATTHEW 24:31 NLT

The prophet Elijah was carried to heaven by a fiery chariot in the midst of a whirlwind (2 Kings 2:11), hence the wording of the following song. But for all the rest of us, it's angels who carry us home.

> *I looked over Jordan, and what did I see*
> *Coming for to carry me home?*
> *A band of angels coming after me,*
> *Coming for to carry me home.*

CHORUS
Swing low, sweet chariot
Coming for to carry me home,
Swing low, sweet chariot,
Coming for to carry me home.

"SWING LOW, SWEET CHARIOT"
BY WALLACE WILLIS, BEFORE 1862

JESUS WILL COMFORT US

Death is a glorious event to one going
to Jesus. Whither does the soul wing
its way? What does it see first? There is
something sublime in passing into the
second stage of our immortal lives
if washed from our sins.
DAVID LIVINGSTONE

When we arrive in heaven we'll be comforted by Jesus Christ, the Lamb of God who died to save us, and who rose victorious from the grave. He will wipe away every tear from our eyes and lead us to fountains of living water.

And we will be with Him forever.

> *"Therefore they are before the throne*
> *of God, and serve Him day and night*
> *in His temple. And He who sits on the*
> *throne will dwell among them. They*
> *shall neither hunger anymore nor thirst*
> *anymore; the sun shall not strike them,*
> *nor any heat; for the Lamb who is in the*
> *midst of the throne will shepherd them*
> *and lead them to living fountains of*
> *waters. And God will wipe*
> *away every tear from their eyes."*
> REVELATION 7:15–17 NKJV

> *Here bring your wounded hearts,*
> *here tell your anguish; earth has no*
> *sorrow that heaven cannot heal.*
> THOMAS MORE

WE DON'T FEAR DEATH

Country musician Buck Owens wrote the song "Tired of Living," in which he confessed that he was tired of livin' and scared of dyin'. As Christians, however, we don't need to fear death.

> *I'll not fear when I pass through the valley,*
> *Though encompassed by shadows of night,*
> *For I know that beyond it is shining*
> *An eternal and glorious light.*

"BEYOND THE SHADOWS"
BY CHARLES W. NAYLOR, BEFORE 1911

It is certain that we all must die—unless Jesus returns first and takes us to heaven. But even though our bodies will one day perish, we need not be anxious.

> *He whose head is in heaven need not*
> *fear to put his feet into the grave.*
> MATTHEW HENRY

Why can we have such confidence in the face of death? Because if we believe in Jesus, death is merely the gateway to heaven. Jesus has taken the sting out of dying. He has snatched away victory from the tomb. As the Bible triumphantly asks, "O death, where is thy sting? O grave, where is thy victory?" (1 Corinthians 15:55 KJV). Small wonder then that Paul declared, "For to me, to live is Christ, and to die is gain" (Philippians 1:21 NKJV).

> *If to die is but to enter into*
> *uninterrupted communion with Jesus,*
> *then death is indeed gain and the black*
> *drop is swallowed up in a sea of victory.*
> CHARLES SPURGEON

REUNIONS WITH OUR LOVED ONES

For many people, the most wonderful prospect of heaven is not only that they will they never be sick or sorrowful again, but that they'll be reunited forever with their departed loved ones.

Though sickness, or trouble, or even
death itself, should come to our house,
and claim our dearest ones, still they are
not lost, but only gone before.
D. L. MOODY

The famous bluegrass/country song, "Will the Circle Be Unbroken?" released on a 1972 album, but few know that it was inspired by a hymn written sixty-five years earlier. Here are some of the original words:

There are loved ones in the glory
Whose dear forms you often miss.
When you close your earthly story,
Will you join them in their bliss?

REFRAIN
Will the circle be unbroken
By and by, Lord, by and by?
There's better home awaiting
In the sky, Lord, in the sky.

"WILL THE CIRCLE BE UNBROKEN?"
BY ADA RUTH HABERSHON, 1907

Fanny Crosby (1820–1915) likewise wrote about the joyous reunions that believers could expect in the next world:

> *On the happy, golden shore,*
> *Where the faithful part no more,*
> *When the storms of life are o'er, meet me*
>   *there;*
> *Where the night dissolves away*
> *Into pure and perfect day,*
> *I am going home to stay, meet me there.*
>
> REFRAIN
> *Meet me there, meet me there,*
> *(Meet me there, meet me there)*
> *Where the tree of life is blooming, meet me*
>   *there;*
> *When the storms of life are o'er,*
> *On the happy golden shore,*
> *Where the faithful part no more, meet me*
>   *there.*

"MEET ME THERE"
BY FANNY J. CROSBY, PUBLISHED 1885

The eastern gate of Jerusalem was the gate that faced the sunrise. A person standing by this gate was the first to see the sun rise over the Mount of Olives in the east, and the beautiful hymn that follows describes two Christians hoping to meet at the eastern gate of the heavenly Jerusalem.

> *If you hasten off to glory,*
> *Linger near the Eastern Gate,*
> *For I'm coming in the morning,*
> *So you'll not have long to wait.*
>
> *I will meet you in the morning*
> *I will meet you in the morning*
> *Just inside the Eastern Gate over there.*

"Eastern Gate" by
Isaiah G. Martin, 1905

Many believe that when they arrive in heaven, the very *first* people to greet them will be their departed loved ones. The Bible doesn't specifically say this, but it's certainly believable. We know that the angels of heaven are well informed about what happens here on earth: they know when we're saved (Luke 15:10), and when our body dies they're there to bring us to heaven. It would be a small thing for them to inform our loved ones so they can greet us as we enter paradise.

IS THERE MARRIAGE IN HEAVEN?

While we often long to see departed parents or friends, for many of us, the greatest joy will be to be reunited with a beloved spouse who has gone to heaven before us. And the question is, "Will we still be married in heaven?" Despite what certain religions teach, the answer is no. In Luke 20:27–33, some religious leaders told Jesus about a woman who'd been married seven times, taking one husband after another after each had died. They then asked Jesus whose wife she would be in the kingdom of God—since she had been married to all seven of them.

Jesus replied, "The people of this age marry and are given in marriage. But

> *those who are considered worthy of*
> *taking part in the age to come and in the*
> *resurrection from the dead will neither*
> *marry nor be given in marriage, and*
> *they can no longer die; for they are like*
> *the angels. They are God's children, since*
> *they are children of the resurrection."*
>
> LUKE 20:34–36 NIV

We'll undoubtedly feel a tender love for those who were our marriage partners on earth, enjoy a special bond with them, and spend a great deal of time in their company—but we will no longer be involved in a marriage union. Instead, the Bible tells us that we'll all be married in spirit to Jesus (see chapter 6).

FELLOWSHIP IN HEAVEN

We will also want to spend time in the company of great men and women of the Bible. Many Christians have said that they'd like to chat with the patriarchs or ask flawed heroes like King David why he did what he did, both

good and bad. Will we get the opportunity?
The Bible says:

> *"And I say to you that many will come
> from east and west, and sit down with
> Abraham, Isaac, and Jacob in the
> kingdom of heaven."*
> MATTHEW 8:11 NKJV

It would take these great men just about
forever to spend time with every single person
who wanted to talk to them—so maybe these
gatherings will be large group events. Perhaps,
to spare them from answering the same questions over and over again, God will simply allow
us to view documentaries of their lives. On the
other hand, we actually *do* have forever to get
to know other believers—and not just the most
celebrated Bible characters.

ARE THERE PETS IN HEAVEN?

Many people believe that their beloved pets go
to heaven when they die. *All Dogs Go to Heaven*

was the title of a 1989 animated movie. But what's the truth of the matter? Not even wise King Solomon knew. He stated:

> *"All go to the same place; all come from dust, and to dust all return. Who knows if the human spirit rises upward and if the spirit of the animal goes down into the earth?"*
>
> ECCLESIASTES 3:20–21 NIV

But other famous men through history have ventured their opinion on this issue:

> *You think dogs will not be in heaven?*
> *I tell you, they will be there*
> *long before any of us.*
>
> ROBERT LOUIS STEVENSON

Personal opinions aside, there *is* an answer in the scriptures. The Bible tells us that there will be animals—such as wolves, sheep, cattle, bears, leopards, snakes—when Jesus is ruling the earth (Isaiah 11:1–9). This is commonly thought to be during the Millennium. But at the *end* of the Millennium, God will destroy the old world and create a new earth. Heaven will be on earth after this point (Revelation 21:1–3), so the question is: Will there still be animals around *then*? The answer is yes. God told the prophet Isaiah,

> *"Look! I am creating new heavens and*
> *a new earth, and no one will even think*
> *about the old ones anymore. . . . The*
> *wolf and the lamb will feed together.*
> *The lion will eat hay like a cow. But the*
> *snakes will eat dust. In those days no*
> *one will be hurt or destroyed*
> *on my holy mountain."*
> ISAIAH 65:17, 25 NLT

Animals such as wolves, sheep, cattle, and snakes will still be around during the days of heaven on earth. Furthermore, Revelation 19:11 and 14 tell us that there are vast herds of horses in heaven. Dogs aren't specifically mentioned, but I think we can safely assume that if even wolves are there, dogs will be, too. As a renowned evangelist said,

God will prepare everything for our
perfect happiness in heaven, and if
it takes my dog being there,
I believe he'll be there.
BILLY GRAHAM

2.

THE REALITY OF HEAVEN

Let's pause now and examine how *real* heaven is. While all the verses we've quoted are true, many modern people have difficulty believing in a spiritual world. Even some Christians tend to think that the Bible's description of heaven is so symbolic and so indefinite that there's no telling whether it exists in any real, tangible way. So let's start at the beginning.

WHERE IS HEAVEN?

Is there actually an indescribably beautiful spiritual realm where the Lord Himself dwells? Is it literally populated by exalted spiritual beings called angels? Is heaven a solid reality, or is it just some ethereal concept? Is the hope of the afterlife, as the skeptics insist, simply a nebulous, pie-in-the-sky hope? And where *is* heaven? These are real questions that require serious answers.

Heaven is almost invariably thought of as being somewhere *above* us. The apostle Paul said, "I was caught up to the third heaven. . . . I was caught up to paradise" (2 Corinthians 12:2, 4 NLT). Paul also referred to the heavenly city as "the Jerusalem above" (Galatians 4:26 NKJV). But where exactly is it? And what exactly did Paul mean by "the *third* heaven"?

The Bible speaks of "heaven" in three different ways: the first heaven is the sky, the earth's atmosphere:

> *And God said, Let the waters bring forth abundantly the moving creature that*

> *hath life, and fowl that may fly above*
> *the earth in the open firmament*
> *of heaven.*
> GENESIS 1:20 KJV

The second heaven is the vastness of outer space where the stars are:

> *"You made the heavens, even the highest*
> *heavens, and all their starry host."*
> NEHEMIAH 9:6 NIV

The third heaven, which is *beyond* these, is paradise, where God dwells. As Moses prayed:

> *"Look down from heaven,*
> *your holy dwelling place,*
> *and bless your people Israel."*
> DEUTERONOMY 26:15 NIV

Is Heaven "In the Clouds"?

Many people have the idea that heaven is some indefinite dreamscape of fluffy clouds. This rather unappealing idea of heaven is of floating weightlessly on cottony clouds, playing harps. This conclusion may be a misinterpretation of verses about Christ's return to earth when He gathers the saved together.

"And they will see the Son of Man coming on the clouds of heaven."
MATTHEW 24:30 NLT

Behold, he cometh with clouds; and every eye shall see him.
REVELATION 1:7 KJV

Then we who are alive and remain shall be caught up together with them in the clouds to meet the Lord in the air.
1 THESSALONIANS 4:17 NKJV

These verses say that when Jesus returns, He will appear above the earth. We who live in that day will meet Him "in the clouds. . .in the air." But that's not our *destination*—it's simply where we'll rendezvous with Him. Once we have joined Him, Jesus takes us to heaven.

HEAVEN—ABOVE THE STARS

Many Christians believe that heaven is somewhere out among the stars, some unfathom-
able distance away. Job asked, "'Is not God in
the height of heaven?'" (Job 22:12 NKJV). Yes,
He is—but *how* high up and how far out, no
one knows. The following hymn, written two
and a half centuries ago, places it beyond the
edges of our solar system:

> *Absent from flesh! then rise, my soul,*
> *Where feet nor wings could never climb,*
> *Beyond the heav'ns, where planets roll,*
> *Measuring the cares and joys of time.*

"ABSENT FROM FLESH! O BLISSFUL THOUGHT!"
BY ISAAC WATTS, BEFORE 1748

The following hundred-year-old hymn
speculatively places the heavenly city among
the stars:

> *There's a city of light 'mid the stars,*
> *   we are told,*

Where they know not a sorrow or care;
And the gates are of pearl,
   and the streets are of gold,
And the building exceedingly fair.

"THE CITY OF LIGHT"
BY A. S. KIEFFER, PUBLISHED 1911

Other Christians believe that heaven is even farther out—beyond the most distant edge of the physical universe. The idea that God's throne is "above" the stars is hinted at in this description of the devil's futile ambition: "For you have said in your heart: 'I will ascend into heaven, I will exalt my throne above the stars of God'" (Isaiah 14:13 NKJV). However, the "stars of God" *here* are an allegorical reference to angels. God asked Job, "'Where were you when I laid the foundations of the earth? . . . When the morning stars sang together, and all the sons of God shouted for joy?'" (Job 38:4, 7 NKJV).

How Far Is Heaven?

So how far away *is* heaven? Many Christians have traditionally assumed that the following verse is describing Jesus and the kingdom of heaven:

> *Thine eyes shall see the king in his*
> *beauty: they shall behold the land*
> *that is very far off.*
> ISAIAH 33:17 KJV

However, the famous preacher Charles Spurgeon (1834–1892) disagreed with this interpretation, saying:

> *Between earth and heaven*
> *there is but a thin partition.*
> *Heaven is much nearer than we think.*
> *I question if "the land*
> *that is very far off"*
> *is a true name for heaven.*
> *as it not an extended kingdom*
> *on earth that was intended*
> *by the prophet rather than*

> *the celestial home? Heaven is*
> *by no means the far country,*
> *for it is the Father's house.*
> CHARLES SPURGEON

Dwight L. Moody (1837–1899) was of a similar opinion:

> *We talk about heaven being so far away.*
> *It is within speaking distance to*
> *those who belong there.*
> DWIGHT L. MOODY

The scriptures seem to bear this out. Paul said that God "'is not far from any one of us. For in him we live and move and exist'" (Acts 17:27–28 NLT). And David said in the psalms:

> *Where can I go from your Spirit? Where*
> *can I flee from your presence? If I go up*
> *to the heavens, you are there; if I make*
> *my bed in the depths, you are there.*
> PSALM 139:7–8 NIV

GOD LIVES IN ETERNITY

King Solomon, the wisest man who ever lived, said of God that "heaven and the heaven of heavens cannot contain Him" (2 Chronicles 2:6 NKJV). The evidence, therefore, points to the fact that God inhabits a timeless spiritual dimension outside of—but coexisting with— our present space-time continuum.

> *For thus says the High and Lofty One*
> *Who inhabits eternity,*
> *whose name is Holy:*
> *"I dwell in the high and holy place,*
> *with him who has a contrite*
> *and humble spirit."*
> ISAIAH 57:15 NKJV

So where is this "high and holy place" where eternity rules and time has no meaning? In modern terms, we would say that God and the inhabitants of heaven are in another dimension.

Heaven in Another Dimension

Scientists used to state with utter certainty that there were only four dimensions: length, height, width, and time. Together these were known as *space-time*. Christians and other spiritually-minded people insisted that there was a fifth dimension, the spiritual realm. It couldn't be perceived with our limited senses because it was above and beyond the plane of four-dimensional physical matter.

> 'Mid the rapturous glories of heaven,
> On immortal and beautiful plane,
> All the ransomed will joyfully gather,
> Nevermore to part again.

"Joyful Meeting in Glory"
by Daniel S. Warner, published 1911

Secular scientists, however, argued that this temporal physical world was the entire reality—that the Christian's hope of unending life in heaven was born merely of a childish fear of dying. But God tells us differently:

"I am the LORD, the Maker of all things,
who stretches out the heavens, who
spreads out the earth by myself. . .who
overthrows the learning of the wise and
turns it into nonsense."

ISAIAH 44:24–25 NIV

Sure enough, in the late 1960s these same skeptics, in their effort to understand how our universe works, came to the astonishing conclusion that reality consisted of no less than *twenty-six* dimensions containing unphysical particle states, all coexisting with our four-dimensional physical realm. This, the "bosonic string theory," was later downgraded to eleven dimensions, seven of which are "rolled up" at the subatomic level.

Other physicists postulate that the matter and energy that make up our visible universe account for only 4 percent of all matter and energy. They theorize that unseen "dark" matter makes up 96 percent of our universe. The fact that this unphysical matter is not detectable doesn't bother them. It makes sense mathematically, seems to explain why gravity is so "weak," and is therefore accepted. Other physicists, however, reject this theory. They propose that hypothetical "gravitons" produce gravity in another dimension and that small amounts of it leak into our reality from there.

Please stay with me for a moment. . .

Still other theoretical physicists now speculate that when the so-called "Big Bang" occurred, its expansion happened at different speeds—causing an almost infinite number of "multiverses," like self-contained bubbles, to come into being. They theorize that separate universes formed, likely with different laws governing their matter and energy.

Here's the point: As unbelievable as some of these hypotheses sound to the average person—and even to other physicists—some of the world's most respected, intelligent thinkers take them seriously. Yet they deny the possibility of a single *spiritual* dimension.

> *As the Scriptures say, "I will destroy
> the wisdom of the wise and discard
> the intelligence of the intelligent." So
> where does this leave the philosophers,*

> *the scholars, and the world's brilliant*
> *debaters? God has made the wisdom*
> *of this world look foolish.*
> 1 CORINTHIANS 1:18–21 NLT

This is not to say that these multidimensional theories aren't true. The point here is that the theoreticians have come a *long* way since the days when they insisted we lived in a simple, four-dimensional universe.

A CONFIDENT HOPE

Paul asked King Agrippa, "'Why does it seem incredible to any of you that God can raise the dead?'" (Acts 26:8 NLT). Given what physicists believe, we may ask, "Why does it seem incredible that there is an eternal, omnipotent God who created all this? Why does it seem incredible that He exists undetected by mortal eyes in another dimension? Why does it seem incredible that God can transform mortals into immortals, and give them eternal life?" The Christian's hope is quite reasonable.

"I am not insane, most excellent Festus,"
Paul replied. "What I am saying is
true and reasonable."
ACTS 26:25 NIV

We can trust the Word of God. We can trust the words of Jesus. He hasn't given us false promises. He would have told us if heaven weren't true. In fact, Jesus said, "'In My Father's house are many mansions; if it were not so, I would have told you'" (John 14:2 NKJV).

So God has given both his promise
and his oath. These two things are
unchangeable because it is impossible
for God to lie. Therefore, we who have
fled to him for refuge can have great
confidence as we hold to the hope that
lies before us. This hope is a strong and
trustworthy anchor for our souls. It
leads us through the curtain into God's
inner sanctuary.
HEBREWS 6:18–19 NLT

The good news is that we don't have to understand theoretical physics to respond to the spiritual hunger we feel inside.

Have you not felt yearnings after the Infinite—hungerings which bread cannot satisfy, thirstings which a river could not quench? Well then, if you have such longings as these, surely there must be a provision to meet them. With my thirstings, my longings, my mysterious instincts, there is a God somewhere; there is a heaven somewhere, there is an atonement somewhere, there is a fullness somewhere to meet my emptiness. Man wants a shelter; there must be a shelter.

CHARLES SPURGEON

3.

GLIMPSES OF HEAVEN

The Windows of Heaven

Scripture passages such as 2 Kings 7:2 and Malachi 3:10 refer to God opening up "the windows of heaven" to pour out His blessings on the earth. Some people think that angels and departed saints in heaven can look through these "windows" and watch us here on earth. This interpretation, however, is likely to be more poetic than real.

The Hebrew word used here for "window" is *arubbah*, which can indicate a window as we know it—though some scholars say the precise meaning is "crevices." In other words, God has promised to create openings in the heavens. Isaiah exclaimed to God, "Oh, that You would rend the heavens! That You would come down!" (Isaiah 64:1 NKJV). In other words, that God would create an opening in the space-time fabric and enter our world from the heavenly dimension. That is precisely what God has done on occasion: "He opened the heavens and came down" (Psalm 18:9 NLT).

HEAVEN OPENED

Several times in the history of the world God has opened the heavens and come through into our dimension:

> *In my thirtieth year. . .while I was*
> *among the exiles by the Kebar River,*
> *the heavens were opened and I saw*
> *visions of God.*
> EZEKIEL 1:1 NIV

This familiar scripture passage describes heaven opening when Jesus was baptized by John in the Jordan River:

> *When He had been baptized, Jesus came*
> *up immediately from the water; and*
> *behold, the heavens were opened to*
> *Him, and He saw the Spirit of God*
> *descending like a dove and alighting*
> *upon Him.*
> MATTHEW 3:16 NKJV

When God opens the heavens and comes to earth, we're given a glimpse of paradise itself—for God is the very center of heaven, the One on whom all the celestial hosts are focused.

GOD IS THE HEART OF HEAVEN

Throughout the Bible, from the Old Testament to the New, prophets describe heaven, the glory of God, angels, cherubim, seraphim, and departed believers. Men such as Moses, Isaiah, Ezekiel, and Daniel were given glimpses of God and the next world—culminating in the grand, detailed panorama John viewed in the book of Revelation, where the magnificence of our everlasting home was laid out before his eyes.

Remember, when the Bible describes the throne room of God and God Himself, we are glimpsing the very heart of heaven. Jesus said, "'Blessed are the pure in heart, for they shall see God'" (Matthew 5:8 NKJV). As Charles Spurgeon asked, "What is heaven, but to be with God, to dwell with Him, to realize that God is mine, and I am His?"

> *The principal happiness of heaven is being with the Lord, seeing Him, living with Him, and enjoying Him forever.*
> MATTHEW HENRY

GOD ON HIS THRONE

The first time the Bible records God appearing on earth in His glory was on Mount Sinai:

*Then Moses, Aaron, Nadab, Abihu,
and the seventy elders of Israel climbed
up the mountain. There they saw the
God of Israel. Under his feet there
seemed to be a surface of brilliant blue
lapis lazuli, as clear as the sky itself.*

EXODUS 24:9–10 NLT

Many centuries later, God once again opened the heavens, this time appearing to the prophet Isaiah:

*In the year that King Uzziah died, I saw
the Lord, high and exalted, seated on a
throne; and the train of his robe filled
the temple. Above him were seraphim,
each with six wings: With two wings
they covered their faces, with two they
covered their feet, and with two they
were flying.*

ISAIAH 6:1–2 NIV

REFRAIN
*Face to face I shall behold Him,
Far beyond the starry sky;*

Face to face in all His glory,
I shall see Him by and by!

"FACE TO FACE"
BY CARRIE E. BRECK, 1898

About one hundred years after Isaiah saw God, the Lord appeared to the prophet Ezekiel:

Then I looked, and behold, a whirlwind
was coming out of the north, a great
cloud with raging fire engulfing itself;
and brightness was all around it and
radiating out of its midst like the color
of amber, out of the midst of the fire.
Also from within it came the likeness
of four living creatures. . . . And above
the firmament over their heads was
the likeness of a throne, in appearance
like a sapphire stone; on the likeness
of the throne was a likeness with the
appearance of a man high above it.
Also from the appearance of His waist
and upward I saw, as it were, the color

of amber with the appearance of fire
all around within it; and from the
appearance of His waist and downward
I saw, as it were, the appearance of fire
with brightness all around. Like the
appearance of a rainbow in a cloud on
a rainy day, so was the appearance of
the brightness all around it. This was the
appearance of the likeness of the glory of
the Lord.
Ezekiel 1:4–5, 26–28 nkjv

At about the same time, the prophet Daniel had a vision of God's throne room:

I beheld till the thrones were cast
down, and the Ancient of days did sit,
whose garment was white as snow, and
the hair of his head like the pure wool:
his throne was like the fiery flame, and
his wheels as burning fire. A fiery stream
issued and came forth from before
him: thousand thousands ministered
unto him, and ten thousand times ten

> *thousand stood before him:*
> *the judgment was set, and the*
> *books were opened.*
> DANIEL 7:9–10 KJV

JESUS ENTHRONED IN HEAVEN

As his vision continued, Daniel saw something astonishing—a Son of man coming with the clouds of heaven. This was none other than Jesus Christ, the Son of God. Jesus used this same expression to describe Himself, saying that "they shall see the Son of man coming in the clouds of heaven with power and great glory" (Matthew 24:30 KJV). Daniel tells us:

> *I saw in the night visions, and, behold,*
> *one like the Son of man came with*
> *the clouds of heaven, and came to the*
> *Ancient of days, and they brought*
> *him near before him. And there was*
> *given him dominion, and glory, and*
> *a kingdom, that all people, nations,*
> *and languages, should serve him: his*
> *dominion is an everlasting dominion,*

> *which shall not pass away,*
> *and his kingdom that which*
> *shall not be destroyed.*
> DANIEL 7:13–14 KJV

The New Testament tells us that after Jesus died and was resurrected, He ascended into heaven and sat down at the right hand of His Father's throne.

> *So then after the Lord had spoken unto*
> *them, he was received up into heaven,*
> *and sat on the right hand of God.*
> MARK 16:19 KJV

> *This is the same mighty power that*
> *raised Christ from the dead and seated*
> *him in the place of honor at God's right*
> *hand in the heavenly realms.*
> EPHESIANS 1:19–20 NLT

> *We do have such a high priest,*
> *who sat down at the right hand of*
> *the throne of the Majesty in heaven.*
> HEBREWS 8:1 NIV

The right hand of the throne of God is *part* of God's throne. Jesus said, "'I also overcame and sat down with My Father on His throne'" (Revelation 3:21 NKJV). Jesus Christ is worthy to sit on God's throne with Him because, as the Nicene Creed states, He *is* God.

> *We believe in one Lord, Jesus Christ,*
> *the only Son of God,*
> *eternally begotten of the Father,*
> *God from God, Light from Light,*
> *true God from true God,*
> *begotten, not made,*
> *one in Being with the Father.*
> THE NICENE CREED

This is why Christians down through the ages have not only worshipped God the Father, but Jesus—God the Son. And as Jon Courson said in *Application Commentary*, "Jesus is what makes heaven heaven."

> *But who can tell us the majesty of Christ?*
> *When He was enthroned in the highest*
> *heavens, He was very God of very God;*

by Him were the heavens made, and
all the hosts of it. His own almighty
arm upheld the spheres, the praises of
cherubim and seraphim perpetually
surrounded Him, the full chorus of the
hallelujahs of the universe unceasingly
flowed to the foot of His throne—He
reigned supreme above all His creatures,
God over all, blessed forever.

CHARLES SPURGEON

While Jesus was still on earth, He longed for His followers to be with Him in heaven, and for them to see the splendor that God the Father had given Him. He prayed:

"Father, I want those you have given me
to be with me where I am, and to see
my glory, the glory you have given me
because you loved me before the
creation of the world."

JOHN 17:24 NIV

One day we shall indeed see Jesus in His full glory, because "when Christ appears. . .we shall see him as he is" (1 John 3:2 NIV).

John's Vision of Heaven

In 95 AD, in New Testament times, the apostle John was caught up to heaven, and he too saw the throne of God:

> *At once I was in the Spirit, and there before me was a throne in heaven with someone sitting on it. And the one who sat there had the appearance of jasper and ruby. A rainbow that shone like an emerald encircled the throne. Surrounding the throne were twenty-four other thrones, and seated on them were twenty-four elders. They were dressed in white and had crowns of gold on their heads. From the throne came flashes of lightning, rumblings and peals of thunder.*
>
> REVELATION 4:2–5 NIV

And there, in the midst of the throne of God in heaven, stood Jesus—identified in chapter 5 as the Lamb of God. Then the four, fearsome living beasts (the cherubim) and the twenty-four elders who had been praising God, fell down and worshipped Jesus. And all the millions upon millions of angels gathered around God's throne also worshipped the Son of God.

> *Read Revelation 5 until your heart is possessed by the thought that all heaven falls prostrate before Christ, and the elders cast their crowns before the throne. The Lamb reigns amid the praises and the love of His ransomed ones and the praises of all creation.*
> ANDREW MURRAY

Jesus is one with God His Father, and is "the brightness of his glory, and the express image of his person" (Hebrews 1:3 KJV). Therefore the greatest joy we'll experience in heaven will be to see Jesus face-to-face, in all of His glorious beauty.

> *When, by the gift of His infinite grace,*
> *I am accorded in Heaven a place,*

Just to be there and to look on His face,
Will through the ages be glory for me.

Friends will be there I have loved long ago;
Joy like a river around me will flow;
Yet just a smile from my Savior, I know,
Will through the ages be glory for me.

CHORUS

O that will be glory for me,
Glory for me, glory for me,
When by His grace I shall look on His face,
That will be glory, be glory for me.

"O THAT WILL BE GLORY"
BY CHARLES H. GABRIEL, 1900

PRAISING GOD FOR ALL ETERNITY

Just as the four cherubim, the twenty-four elders, and all the millions of angels worship God and Jesus Christ, the Lamb of God, we, too, will worship.

> *After this I looked, and there before me*
> *was a great multitude that no one could*
> *count, from every nation, tribe, people and*
> *language, standing before the throne and*
> *before the Lamb. They were wearing white*
> *robes and were holding palm branches in*
> *their hands. And they cried out in a loud*
> *voice: "Salvation belongs to our God, who*
> *sits on the throne, and to the Lamb."*
>
> REVELATION 7:9–10 NIV

And this won't just be a one-time event. As the hymn "Amazing Grace" tells us:

> *When we've been there ten thousand years,*
> *Bright shining as the sun,*
> *We've no less days to sing God's praise*
> *Than when we'd first begun.*
>
> "AMAZING GRACE," FINAL STANZA
> ADDED TO JOHN NEWTON'S WORK, 1829

In fact, for the four living creatures surrounding God's throne, praising Him is a full-time vocation:

> *The four living creatures. . .do not rest*
> *day or night, saying: "Holy, holy, holy,*
> *Lord God Almighty, Who was and is*
> *and is to come!"*
> REVELATION 4:8 NKJV

Praising the Lord will be our chief joy in heaven as well, so it makes sense that we should enjoy praising Him here and now on earth.

> *Praise is the work and happiness of*
> *heaven, and all who would go to heaven*
> *must begin their heaven now.*
> MATTHEW HENRY

IS HEAVEN BORING?

For many people, particularly non-Christians, the thought of waving palm fronds, strumming harps, and singing praise to God forever doesn't sound very appealing. Even many Christians, if they're honest, will admit that they might find the idea appealing in small doses—say, an hour or so every Sunday—but wouldn't like to do solely that forever.

In 1909, Mark Twain published "Captain Stormfield's Visit to Heaven," a satire that poked fun at stereotypical concepts of heaven. While much of what Twain wrote was unscriptural, parts of his story were thought-provoking. He humorously described Captain Stormfield, a new arrival in heaven, requesting the harp, halo, and hymnbook he believed he needed, then proceeding to the nearest cloud bank on his new wings to join millions of others in creating a joyful but utterly discordant noise. After a while, Stormfield came back down and asked a friend:

> *"Now tell me—is this to go on forever?*
> *Ain't there anything else for a change?"*
> MARK TWAIN

Certainly we will praise the Lord in heaven. And considering the fact that we'll be face-to-face with the eternal Creator Himself, we won't find it boring. God is transcendently beautiful and glorious, and seeing Him in person will make for spontaneous adoration. Worshipping God will likely give us rapturous pleasure, and we'll have a hard time tearing our eyes away from Him. Few people here on earth have had such an encounter with God, or experienced the magnificence of His presence—but in heaven we'll *all* have that privilege.

> *One thing I have desired of the LORD,*
> *that will I seek: that I may dwell in the*
> *house of the LORD all the days of my life,*
> *to behold the beauty of the LORD,*
> *and to inquire in His temple.*
>
> PSALM 27:4 NKJV

EXPLORING AND LEARNING FOR ETERNITY

We'll also have an eternity in which to do myriad other things. After we've learned everything we could possibly wish to know about heaven and our own world, we'll be able to explore new worlds. It will take us quite some time to explore the entire Milky Way galaxy, and even *that's* not the end! There are an estimated 170 billion galaxies in the universe, and only God knows how many universes there are. There will be an eternity of things to experience and learn.

Some people have the impression that once we get to heaven we'll instantly know everything—just like God does. They base the idea upon this verse: "For now we see through a glass, darkly; but then face to face: now I know in part; but then shall I know even as also I am known" (1 Corinthians 13:12 KJV). But this isn't saying we'll be instantly omniscient. It means that—just as God knows *us* for who we are right now—when we come face-to-face with Him, we'll see Him in His full, unveiled glory, knowing Him as He truly is, as God Almighty.

We'll have lots to learn, which is one reason that we'll "inquire," as the psalm writer says. We will ask God questions. Remember, even the angels who have lived in heaven for untold millennia don't know everything. They don't know the day that Jesus will return (Mark 13:32), for example. So they ask questions. And many of these questions aren't mere intellectual inquiries, but rather—like many of our prayers—emotional cries to God about why He allows certain situations.

> *Upon hearing this, the angel of the Lord*
> *prayed this prayer: "O Lord of Heaven's*
> *Armies, for seventy years now you have*
> *been angry with Jerusalem and the*
> *towns of Judah. How long until you*
> *again show mercy to them?" And the*
> *Lord spoke kind and comforting words*
> *to the angel who talked with me.*
> ZECHARIAH 1:12–13 NLT

How well we understand such questions! How we ourselves long for the Lord to speak kind and comforting words to us concerning situations we've endured. And one day all our questions *will* be answered.

HAPPINESS AND LAUGHTER IN HEAVEN

Mark Twain also expressed many people's misgivings about the kingdom of God when he complained, "There is no humor in heaven." But this isn't true. Jesus himself said:

> *"Blessed are you who are poor, for yours*
> *is the kingdom of God. Blessed are*
> *you who hunger now, for you will be*
> *satisfied. Blessed are you who weep now,*
> *for you will laugh."*
> LUKE 6:20–21 NIV

Certainly, the great reformer Martin Luther had no view of heaven. He bluntly stated:

> *If you are not allowed to laugh in*
> *heaven, I don't want to go there.*
> MARTIN LUTHER

You can be sure that there is plenty of laughter in heaven.

4.

THE KINGDOM OF HEAVEN

Jesus said, "'Father, I want those you have given me to be with me where I am'" (John 17:24 NIV). Jesus wanted us to see Him in His glory, but He also wished to share heaven with us. The Bible tells us that all things belonging to God also belong to His Son. Jesus declared, "'All things that the Father has are Mine'" (John 16:15 NKJV). Christ is heir to all that God has.

But we are told the surprising news that *we* are also heirs of God (Galatians 4:7), and that all things in heaven belong to us, as well. So

Jesus not only wants us to see Him in *His* glory, but He wants to reveal His glory in *us* as well.

The Spirit Himself bears witness with
our spirit that we are children of God,
and if children, then heirs—heirs of God
and joint heirs with Christ, if indeed we
suffer with Him, that we may also be
glorified together.
ROMANS 8:16–17 NKJV

What a thought! Jesus desires to share everything in all of heaven with us!

The boundless realms of His Father's
universe are Christ's by prescriptive
right. He is the sole proprietor of the vast
creation of God, and He has admitted us
to claim the whole as ours. The golden
streets of paradise, the pearly gates, the
river of life, the transcendent bliss, and the
unutterable glory are, by our blessed Lord,
offered to us for our everlasting possession.
All that He has, He shares with His people.
CHARLES SPURGEON

THE KINGDOM OF GOD ALREADY

We shall enjoy myriad things in heaven. But as mentioned earlier, our chief happiness will be enjoying the presence of God. This doesn't just mean when we come before His throne and worship, because the Spirit of God will be present within us *wherever* we are in heaven. If God gives us His Spirit while we're in these weak, mortal bodies on earth, how much more will we be filled with His Spirit in the next life? God is in our hearts now—He will fill our lives to overflowing then.

This also explains why we can experience some of the joys of the kingdom of heaven while we're still here on earth. Jesus said:

> *"The kingdom of God does not come with observation; nor will they say, 'See here!' or 'See there!' For indeed, the kingdom of God is within you."*
> LUKE 17:20–21 NKJV

Though this life is often a far cry from paradise, we can get a foretaste of heaven while we live on earth. When we arrive in the ultimate kingdom of God, the curtains will be drawn aside, and we'll see and experience life—life everlasting—in its full splendor.

> *The inward kingdom of heaven,*
> *set up in the hearts of all who repent*
> *and believe the gospel, is righteousness,*
> *peace, and joy in the Holy Spirit.*
> *But these are only the first fruits.*
> *While these blessings are inconceivably*
> *great, yet we trust to see greater.*
> JOHN WESLEY

EATING AND DRINKING IN HEAVEN

Many people wonder whether we'll eat and drink in heaven. It hardly seems necessary, since the reason we do so now is to keep our bodies alive—and in heaven, we'll be enjoying *eternal* life. Some think that the following verse means that we *won't* eat or drink in heaven: "For the kingdom of God is not a matter of eating and drinking, but of righteousness, peace

and joy in the Holy Spirit" (Romans 14:17
NIV). But if you read the verse in context, it be-
comes apparent that the apostle Paul was talking about not judging others for what they eat
and drink in the here and now.

Feasting with others and enjoying delicious
tastes gives us pleasure—and perhaps for these
reasons we *will* both eat and drink in heaven.
Jesus said, "'I will no longer drink of the fruit
of the vine until that day when I drink it new
in the kingdom of God'" (Mark 14:25 NKJV).
So Jesus planned on drinking it in heaven—
though whether this is anything like the "fruit
of the vine" produced here on earth is open to
interpretation. Some Christians suggest that,
in heaven, the water of life is the "wine" we'll
drink.

> *And he showed me a pure river of water
> of life, clear as crystal, proceeding from
> the throne of God and of the Lamb.*
> REVELATION 22:1 NKJV

Juan Ponce de Leon sought a mythical
spring in Florida called the Fountain of

Youth—but he never found it, because it's actually in heaven. In paradise, we will drink the water of life. Jesus promised:

> *I will give unto him that is athirst of the*
> *fountain of the water of life freely.*
> REVELATION 21:6 KJV

And the Holy Spirit calls out:

> *And whosoever will, let him*
> *take the water of life freely.*
> REVELATION 22:17 KJV

After we have tasted the exhilarating water of life, it's doubtful that we'd desire or be satisfied with anything less.

> *Soon will these shadows flee away,*
> *and the day of eternity dawn upon me!*
> *Soon shall I drink of the river of water of*
> *life going out of the throne of God*
> *and of the Lamb!*
> JOHN WESLEY

Eating Angels' Food

Jesus said that "'many will come from east and west, and sit down with Abraham, Isaac, and Jacob in the kingdom of heaven'" (Matthew 8:11 NKJV). This doesn't simply mean they'll simply sit on a bench to chat—they will sit down together as they "'take their places at the feast in the kingdom of God'" (Luke 13:28–29 NIV). Yes, a feast! The Bible tells us:

> *Blessed are they which are called*
> *unto the marriage supper of the Lamb.*
> REVELATION 19:9 KJV

But what will we feast on? What kinds of food will we eat? Well, to start with, Jesus promised, "'To him who overcomes I will give some of the hidden manna to eat'" (Revelation 2:17 NKJV). Now, manna is definitely heavenly food:

> *But he commanded the skies to open;*
> *he opened the doors of heaven.*
> *He rained down manna for them to eat;*

he gave them bread from heaven.
They ate the food of angels!
PSALM 78:23–25 NLT

The Bible indicates that we will also eat from the tree of life which bears twelve different kinds of fruit (Revelation 22:2).

"To him who overcomes I will give to
eat from the tree of life, which is in the
midst of the Paradise of God."
REVELATION 2:7 NKJV

We'll eat manna and different kinds of fruit, but chances are good that these are just *some* of the things on the menu. After all, Jesus ate a variety of food after He rose from the dead and appeared in His eternal resurrection body.

He said to them, "Have you any food
here?" So they gave Him a piece of a
broiled fish and some honeycomb. And
He took it and ate in their presence.
LUKE 24:41–43 NKJV

This wasn't the only time that Jesus ate delicious home-cooked food. Peter declared that he and the other disciples "ate and drank with Him after He arose from the dead" (Acts 10:41 NKJV). Jesus even fried fish and baked bread for them in Galilee (John 21:9–13). If we're eating for enjoyment in heaven, we'll likely consume a wide variety of enjoyable food.

MANSIONS IN HEAVEN

One of Jesus' most well-known promises regarding heaven concerns the eternal dwellings we'll have there. He stated:

> *"In My Father's house are many mansions;*
> *if it were not so, I would have told you. I*
> *go to prepare a place for you. And if I go*
> *and prepare a place for you, I will come*
> *again and receive you to Myself; that*
> *where I am, there you may be also."*
> JOHN 14:2–3 NKJV

Not surprisingly, this promise has inspired believers for the last two thousand years.

And not only those who were accustomed to fine things in this life and were looking for something even *better* in the next—but particularly the poor, the oppressed, the destitute. Many of the great hymns of the past spoke of looking forward to a heavenly mansion:

> *A mansion is waiting in glory,*
> *My Savior has gone to prepare;*
> *The ransomed who shine in its beauty,*
> *Will dwell in that city so fair.*

> *A mansion unclouded by sorrow,*
> *Undimmed by the pains of farewell,*
> *Where all of earth's pilgrims will gather,*
> *With Christ in His glory to dwell.*

"A MANSION IN GLORY"
BY DANIEL S. WARNER, 1911

Many believers have envisioned these "mansions" as sprawling marble palaces, complete with spiral staircases of gold, paradisiacal gardens, fountains, Olympic-sized swimming pools, even angels as servants. However, the

New International Version of the Bible follows the Greek closely in this verse, translating Jesus' statement as, "My Father's house has many rooms" (John 14:2 NIV). That would mean that we won't have our own stand-alone palaces—we'll be living in one, enormous, city-sized palace with a lot of other people. But there's no telling how large and lavish the rooms will be.

> *If one Indian ruler could prepare something as breathtakingly beautiful as the Taj Mahal as a tomb for his wife of just fourteen years, what must God be preparing as a home where He will live forever and ever with His people whom He loves?*

HEAVEN: MY FATHER'S HOUSE
BY ANNE GRAHAM LOTZ

A desire for a heavenly mansion may seem materialistic, but it's not. If we believe God is providing a mansion for us in the next life, we're less inclined to strive for one here and now. We're more likely to hold physical possessions with a loose hand. We're more likely to share our bounty with the poor rather than selfishly hoarding riches. We're more likely to give freely and generously as Jesus commanded.

Jesus said, "Where your treasure is, there will your heart be also" (Matthew 6:21 KJV). Whatever these mansions—or chambers within God's immense mansion—are like, they're *part* of our treasure in heaven, and they are a treasure worth desiring. We are to set our hearts on them, because the greatest palaces on earth are nothing compared to what we'll enjoy in heaven. In fact,

> *To go to heaven, fully to enjoy God, is*
> *infinitely better than the most pleasant*
> *accommodations here.*
> JONATHAN EDWARDS

STREETS OF GOLD

For centuries, the following brief verse has inspired believers—especially impoverished believers who have walked barefoot on dusty dirt roads all their lives. But in modern times, many Christians have wondered if this is actually meant to represent something tangible and real:

> *And the street of the city was pure gold,*
> *like transparent glass.*
> REVELATION 21:21 NKJV

For two millennia, though, Christians have taken the verse at face value, as many hymns of the past testify:

> *There is a wondrous city,*
> *Streets of transparent gold;*
> *Not half its glorious beauty*
> *Has e'er to mortals been told.*

> "OVER YONDER"
> BY HENRY DE FLUITER, 1918

Are the streets of the heavenly city, the new Jerusalem, actually made of pure gold, like transparent glass—or is this simply a metaphor for something? Well, since God Himself dwells in this city, it stands to reason that it would be so

magnificent, made of such extraordinary mate-
rials, that it would make earthly gold and jewels
seem like cheap imitations. Why *wouldn't* the
streets of God's capital be gold—and not only
gold, but supernatural gold as transparent as
glass? If God can change our mortal physical
bodies into glorious bodies that never die and
that shine like the sun, what could He do with
mere gold?

But the streets aren't the only things made
of gold—the entire *city* is composed of the
same amazing, awe-inspiring material. John
tells us that "the city was pure gold, like clear
glass" (Revelation 21:18 NKJV). And here's
something we know for certain:

> *None will walk the celestial pavement of*
> *heaven but those washed in the blood.*
> D. L. MOODY

So yes, God has promised us mansions to
dwell in and streets of gold to walk on. It simply
remains to be seen what form these mansions
and streets will take. Even if, as some argue,
they are metaphors for something else, they

nevertheless represent *tangible* spiritual realities. Whatever picture we have in our minds, the reality we will one day encounter will be even better. Consider this promise:

> *"Eye has not seen, nor ear heard,*
> *nor have entered into the heart*
> *of man the things which God has*
> *prepared for those who love Him."*
> 1 CORINTHIANS 2:9 NKJV

So without any apologies, you can sing the old hymn, "The Mansion Over the Hilltop."

GOD'S GIFTS FOR OVERCOMERS

Jesus made many other promises regarding what Christians will have in heaven. Here are some of those promises:

> *"To him who overcomes I will give*
> *to eat from the tree of life, which is in*
> *the midst of the Paradise of God."*
> REVELATION 2:7 NKJV

*"He who overcomes shall not
be hurt by the second death."*
REVELATION 2:11 NKJV

*"To him who overcomes I will give
some of the hidden manna to eat.
And I will give him a white stone,
and on the stone a new name written
which no one knows except him
who receives it."*
REVELATION 2:17 NKJV

*"And he who overcomes, and keeps
My works until the end, to him I will
give power over the nations. . .and
I will give him the morning star."*
REVELATION 2:26, 28 NKJV

*"He who overcomes shall be clothed in
white garments, and I will not blot out
his name from the Book of Life; but I
will confess his name before My Father
and before His angels."*
REVELATION 3:5 NKJV

"He who overcomes, I will make him a pillar in the temple of My God, and he shall go out no more. I will write on him the name of My God and the name of the city of My God, the New Jerusalem, which comes down out of heaven from My God. And I will write on him My new name."

REVELATION 3:12 NKJV

"To him who overcomes I will grant to sit with Me on My throne, as I also overcame and sat down with My Father on His throne."

REVELATION 3:21 NKJV

Some people believe that "him who over-comes" doesn't refer to *all* Christians, but only to an elite group of victorious, extra-faithful ones who never sin or stumble. But the following passage makes it clear that an *overcomer* is anyone who sincerely believes in Jesus—anyone who has been born again:

> *For whatever is born of God overcomes*
> *the world. And this is the victory that*
> *has overcome the world—our faith.*
> *Who is he who overcomes the world,*
> *but he who believes that Jesus is*
> *the Son of God?*
>
> 1 JOHN 5:4–5 NKJV

Furthermore, overcomers won't only in-herit the above-mentioned promises, but will have free access to *all* that heaven has to offer:

> *He that overcometh shall inherit*
> *all things; and I will be his God,*
> *and he shall be my son.*
>
> REVELATION 21:7 KJV

WHITE ROBES

Many believe that when the Bible describes de-parted believers in heaven as being "clothed in fine linen, white and clean" (Revelation 19:14 KJV), that it's a literal statement: White robes are all that *anyone* wears in heaven. Others believe the descriptions are symbolic. Here is one of the main passages describing heavenly attire:

> *After this I looked, and there before me*
> *was a great multitude that no one could*
> *count. . .standing before the throne and*
> *before the Lamb. They were wearing*
> *white robes and were holding palm*
> *branches in their hands.*
> REVELATION 7:9 NIV

Referring to the worldwide body of believers as the Bride of Christ, the Bible states,

> *And to her was granted that she should*
> *be arrayed in fine linen, clean and white:*
> *for the fine linen is the righteousness*
> *of saints.*
> REVELATION 19:8 KJV

Here, obviously, fine white linen symbolizes the righteousness that allows us to enter into heaven. On our own, we have none. "When we display our righteous deeds, they are nothing but filthy rags" (Isaiah 64:6 NLT). Yet there is cause to rejoice:

> *I will greatly rejoice in the LORD, my*
> *soul shall be joyful in my God; for He*
> *has clothed me with the garments of*
> *salvation, He has covered me with*
> *the robe of righteousness.*
> ISAIAH 61:10 NKJV

God gives us white robes, and He also makes them clean: "'Blessed are those who wash their robes, that they may have the right to the tree of life and may go through the gates into the city'" (Revelation 22:14 NIV). Just how do people wash their robes? John tells us that "they have washed their robes and made them white in the blood of the Lamb" (Revelation 7:14 NIV).

I believe that the Bible's descriptions are intended to be taken at face value whenever possible, and as representing a genuine reality even when symbolic. We will, after all, be wearing *some* kind of extraordinary, unearthly clothing in the next life. Our spirits will be clothed with robes of righteousness, but that doesn't necessarily mean that we'll *also* wear robes on our immortal physical bodies. It could be other forms of attire, whether casual or elegant.

Shall we gather at the river,
Where bright angel feet have trod,
With its crystal tide forever
Flowing by the throne of God?

REFRAIN
Yes, we'll gather at the river,
The beautiful, the beautiful river;
Gather with the saints at the river
That flows by the throne of God.

Ere we reach the shining river,
Lay we every burden down;
Grace our spirits will deliver,
And provide a robe and crown.

"SHALL WE GATHER AT THE RIVER?"
BY ROBERT LOWRY, 1864

HEAVENLY HARPS

Something many Christians wonder about is the common belief that we'll all play harps. . . all the time. While some people actually *like* harp music (in moderation), they wouldn't want to listen to it continuously. Nor do they look forward to *playing* the harp nonstop.

It's true that the twenty-four elders around God's throne have harps (Revelation 5:8). And so do a vast multitude of believers:

> *And I heard a voice from heaven, as the*
> *voice of many waters, and as the voice of*
> *a great thunder: and I heard the voice of*
> *harpers harping with their harps.*
> REVELATION 14:2 KJV

> *And I saw as it were a sea of glass*
> *mingled with fire: and them that had*
> *gotten the victory over the beast. . .*
> *stand on the sea of glass,*
> *having the harps of God.*
> REVELATION 15:2 KJV

These "harps of God" could be either literal or symbolic. Very possibly, they're quite tangible but like nothing we've ever seen or heard on earth. And they may be only used on special occasions, such as at the above-mentioned assemblies before God's throne.

OF WINGS AND ANGELS

The belief that people somehow sprout wings in heaven is based upon a misunderstanding. Many people believe that humans, when they die, become angels. According to TV shows and movies, new arrivals in heaven have to "earn their wings" to become angels. Not so. Angels are a distinct race of beings, created by God before He brought the galaxies into being. Human beings were created last of all. After the resurrection, humans will have glorious bodies and powers *like* angels, but we won't *become* angels. It's a case of apples and oranges. In Revelation 7, John first describes an innumerable multitude of saved humans in heaven (verse 9) then describes a separate multitude of angels (verse 11).

The misconception that people become angels stems, in part, from concern over loved ones. Parents who have watched over their children for years—even when their children are adults—often wish to continue looking out for them after they've gone to heaven. But guarding our loved ones from the spiritual realm is the job of angels.

The angel of the LORD encamps
around those who fear him,
and he delivers them.
PSALM 34:7 NIV

If you make the LORD your refuge. . .
he will order his angels to protect
you wherever you go.
PSALM 91:9–11 NLT

We are not angels—nor will we become angels. God has sent His angels to serve human beings. "Are not all angels ministering spirits sent to serve those who will inherit salvation?" (Hebrews 1:14 NIV). Angels are already immortal and don't inherit the salvation that

92

Christ brings us. They don't even understand how God saves us—though they wish they did (1 Peter 1:12). Nevertheless, "'there is rejoicing in the presence of the angels of God over one sinner who repents'" (Luke 15:10 NIV).

5.

CITIZENSHIP IN HEAVEN

THE WAY TO HEAVEN

After reading about heaven. . .after learning how wonderful and desirable it is. . .how *real* it is. . .you may be looking forward to going there. But how can you be *sure* you're going to heaven when you die? This is, after all, a matter of which you must be absolutely certain.

I want to know one thing—
the way to heaven; how to land
safe on that happy shore.
JOHN WESLEY

You can't leave your eternal destination up to chance. You can't risk it all on some vague hope that because you are "a good, moral person" that you (hopefully!) deserve to go there. The truth is that *none* of us deserve to dwell in the heavenly realm with God. No one is righteous enough to be worthy of heaven (Romans 3:23; 6:23). But the good news is that God *longs* to give you eternal life! It pleases Him greatly! As Jesus said,

> *Fear not, little flock; for it is your*
> *Father's good pleasure to give*
> *you the kingdom.*
> LUKE 12:32 KJV

God created people to live in a perfect world. That's why He placed the first human beings, Adam and Eve, in the Garden of Eden. They sinned and had to leave paradise, but God's will for mankind was not thwarted.

> *Sin has shut us out of Eden; yet let us*
> *not weep, for Christ has prepared a*
> *better paradise for us in heaven. God has*

> *provided for us "a pure river of water of*
> *life" and a lovelier garden than Eden*
> *ever was; and there we shall forever*
> *dwell through the abounding grace of our*
> *Lord and Savior Jesus Christ, which has*
> *abounded even over our abounding sin.*
> CHARLES SPURGEON

So what is this "abounding grace" of Jesus Christ that saves us? Well, *grace* means undeserved favor. Grace is a gift—and it can't be earned. You simply have to reach out your hand of faith to receive salvation of God.

> *For it is by grace you have been saved,*
> *through faith—and this is not from*
> *yourselves, it is the gift of God—not by*
> *works, so that no one can boast.*
> EPHESIANS 2:8–9 NIV

To receive salvation, you must first of all recognize that you're a sinner—that you can't save yourself or earn your way to heaven by doing enough good deeds. You must realize that you need someone to save you from hell.

You need a Savior.

And there *is* a Savior, Jesus Christ, the Son of God. He died on a cross to take your punishment for your sins. You must believe in Him—and Him alone—to save you. "'Nor is there salvation in any other, for there is no other name under heaven given among men by which we must be saved'" (Acts 4:12 NKJV). There *is* a way to heaven, and Jesus tells us, "'I am the way and the truth and the life. No one comes to the Father except through me'" (John 14:6 NIV). And it is important to realize

> *He did not come to save us because we were worth the saving, but because we were utterly worthless, ruined, and undone.*
> CHARLES SPURGEON

Receive Jesus Christ as your Savior, . . . believe that He died for your sins and that He rose again from the dead and lives forevermore, . . .ask Him to come into your heart, . . .and you will be born again. You will be washed from your sins. You will become a son or daughter of God.

THE BOOK OF LIFE

> *You know, eternal life does not start*
> *when you go to heaven. It starts the*
> *moment you reach out to Jesus.*
> *That is where it all begins!*

HE CARES, HE COMFORTS
BY CORRIE TEN BOOM

The moment that you accept Jesus as your Savior, you become spiritually alive. Though you're still on earth, your name is now written in heaven's Book of Life. Your paperwork is already processed. You're already a citizen of heaven. When you do die, you'll automatically be granted entry. This is cause for great celebration! As Jesus told His disciples, "'rejoice that your names are written in heaven'" (Luke 10:20 NIV).

You are now a victorious overcomer, clothed in a robe of righteousness. When you get to heaven, Jesus will announce to His Father that you belong to Him:

*"All who are victorious will be
clothed in white. I will never erase their
names from the Book of Life, but I will
announce before my Father and his
angels that they are mine."*
REVELATION 3:5 NLT

You may freely enter the heavenly city, the
new Jerusalem, if you are one of those "whose
names are written in the Lamb's book of life"
(Revelation 21:27 NIV).

CITIZENS OF HEAVEN

*Good Christians, even while they are
here on earth, are citizens of heaven.
This world is not our home; heaven is.
The life of a Christian is heaven,
where his home is and where
he hopes to be shortly.*
MATTHEW HENRY

We need to understand that although we live on
this earth and are citizens of a certain nation,

we are, first and foremost, citizens of the king-dom of heaven. "For our citizenship is in heaven, from which we also eagerly wait for the Savior, the Lord Jesus Christ" (Philippians 3:20 NKJV). We became citizens of heaven when God adopted us as His sons and daughters.

> *Now, therefore, you are no longer strangers*
> *and foreigners, but fellow citizens with the*
> *saints and members of the household of God.*
> EPHESIANS 2:19 NKJV

This wonderful old hymn reminds us that we have a new homeland and that we are citi-zens of that new country:

> *Come let us sing of homeland,*
> *Down by the crystal sea;*
> *Wonderful land where Jesus*
> *Buildeth a mansion for me.*
>
> *Water of life there floweth,*
> *Fruit in abundant store;*
> *Citizens of that country*
> *Hunger and thirst nevermore.*

REFRAIN
Over yonder, down by the crystal sea,
Over yonder, there's where I long to be;
No more sorrow, toil, grief, nor care,
In that homeland bright and fair,
Over, over there.

"OVER YONDER"
BY HENRY DE FLUITER, 1918

WE ARE FOREIGNERS AND NOMADS

After presenting a long list of Bible heroes who lived and died before Jesus' day, the writer of Hebrews said:

> *These all died in faith, not having*
> *received the promises, but having seen*
> *them afar off, and were persuaded of*
> *them, and embraced them, and confessed*
> *that they were strangers and pilgrims on*
> *the earth. For they that say such things*
> *declare plainly that they seek a country.*
> HEBREWS 11:13–14 KJV

What does it mean to be "strangers and pilgrims on the earth"? The New Living Translation puts it this way: "They agreed that they were foreigners and nomads here on earth." In other words, not "strangers" in the sense of fellow citizens you haven't been introduced to, but *foreigners*—people who stand out as different and don't quite fit into established society. Not only foreigners, but nomads—those having no certain dwelling place. In a very real sense, we are rootless nomads in this world.

This may not seem to describe the millions of Christians who are settled down securely with a thirty-year mortgage—but God has the long view. We're the shortsighted ones. For example, even though the Lord promised the land of Canaan to the Israelites—even though they lived on the land and farmed it—they never truly *owned* it because their lives were so short. They were like flickering shadows just passing over it. God made it clear who *really* owned the land, and what that meant:

> *"The land must never be sold on a
> permanent basis, for the land belongs to
> me. You are only foreigners and tenant
> farmers working for me."*
> LEVITICUS 25:23 NLT

King Solomon, master of an area that
stretched from Egypt to the Euphrates River,
sat on a throne in splendor and grandeur—
but still declared:

> *Vanity of vanities, saith the Preacher,
> vanity of vanities; all is vanity. What
> profit hath a man of all his labour which
> he taketh under the sun? One generation
> passeth away, and another generation
> cometh: but the earth abideth for ever.*
> ECCLESIASTES 1:2–4 KJV

Even the long-lived, immensely wealthy
landowner Job complained, "'my life is but a
breath'" (Job 7:7 NIV). Job bemoaned mankind's lot, saying:

*"How frail is humanity! How short is
life, how full of trouble! We blossom like
a flower and then wither. Like a passing
shadow, we quickly disappear."*
JOB 14:1–2 NLT

We live in this world—but we're not here
long. We pass like a shadow over the land, and
then we're gone. Our ultimate home, our final
forwarding address, is *heaven*. That's why the
Bible cautions us to not love this present world
too much, to allow ourselves to become too at-
tached to it. When it comes down to it, we're
foreigners, nomads, and migrant workers
traveling through this world on our way to an
eternal destination. We must love heaven more
than we love earth.

The love of heaven makes one heavenly.
WILLIAM SHAKESPEARE

HEADED TO A HEAVENLY COUNTRY

God knows it's difficult for our thoughts to be filled with heaven when we're just starting to make our mark in this life. It's easier for those who are older—who have experienced success and failure, known brief joys and prolonged sorrows, and grown weary of what this world has to offer—to have a clearer perspective. But many young people are just as disillusioned with the unfair, dog-eat-dog system of this world, and long for something better. So, whether young or old, Christians are to set their hearts on "a better country."

But now they desire a better country,
that is, an heavenly: wherefore God is
not ashamed to be called their God: for
he hath prepared for them a city.
HEBREWS 11:16 KJV

The better country we desire is heaven, but what city is this that God has prepared for us? It's "the Holy City, the new Jerusalem" (Revelation 21:2 NIV), "the Jerusalem above"

(Galatians 4:26 NKJV). It's the capital of the kingdom of heaven.

> *Heaven is indeed the only home of our souls, and we shall never feel that we have come to our rest until we have reached its mansions.*
> CHARLES SPURGEON

Knowing that our ultimate loyalties are to the kingdom of God will cause us to live according to the laws of His kingdom, even in the here and now. "We should live in this evil world with wisdom, righteousness, and devotion to God" (Titus 2:12 NLT). This knowledge will help us to love our neighbors and obey Christ's commands, even when they're difficult or inconvenient.

> *All who are designed for heaven hereafter are prepared for heaven now. Those who are sanctified and renewed go out of the world with their heaven about them.*
> MATTHEW HENRY

We are therefore to "seek those things which are above, where Christ is, sitting at the right hand of God" (Colossians 3:1 NKJV).

> *Those who are truly filled with the Spirit
> have a heavenly life in themselves. They
> are in daily fellowship with the Father
> and with the Son and seek the things
> that are above. Their main characteristic
> is heavenly-mindedness. They carry
> with them the marks of their eternal,
> heavenly destiny.*
> ANDREW MURRAY

TREASURES IN HEAVEN

> *If you have anything that you prize very
> highly, hold it very loosely for you may
> easily lose it. Hold everything earthly
> with a loose hand, but grasp eternal
> things with a deathlike grip.*
> CHARLES SPURGEON

Once we realize that heaven is our true home, the place where we'll live for eternal ages, we see things in proper perspective. There's really no point in wasting our years, striving to get ahead and focusing on wealth on this earth. We'll just have to leave it all behind soon enough. Real life is more than the accumulation of material things. As Jesus warned,

> *"Watch out! Be on your guard against*
> *all kinds of greed; life does not consist in*
> *an abundance of possessions."*
> LUKE 12:15 NIV

You've probably heard the gleeful saying, "He who dies with the most toys, wins." But the apostle Paul reminds us that that is *not* really winning:

> *For we brought nothing into this world,*
> *and it is certain we can carry nothing out.*
> 1 TIMOTHY 6:7 KJV

With these thoughts firmly in mind—realizing that we are on earth only a short time, and that we'll be in heaven forever—we see that our priorities should be on heavenly things. This is why Jesus told us to store up treasures in heaven, not on earth.

Lay not up for yourselves treasures upon earth, where moth and rust doth corrupt, and where thieves break through and steal: But lay up for yourselves treasures in heaven, where neither moth nor rust doth corrupt, and where thieves do not break through nor steal: For where your treasure is, there will your heart be also.
MATTHEW 6:19–21 KJV

There are many ways to send treasure ahead to heaven—some of the surest include being generous with our love, our time, our possessions, and yes, our money. Jesus advised one overly-materialistic young man, "'If you want to be perfect, go, sell what you have and give to the poor, and you will have treasure in heaven; and come, follow Me'" (Matthew 19:21 NKJV). The young man's heart was so ensnared by riches that Jesus advised a radical solution. He may not ask *you* to give away every earthly thing you own—but the principle of giving still applies if you want treasure in heaven.

> *You will have no reward in heaven for what you lay up; you will for what you lay out. Every dollar you put into the earthly bank is sunk; it brings no interest above. But every dollar you give to the poor is put into the bank of heaven. And it will bring glorious interest, accumulating to all eternity.*
> JOHN WESLEY

We are considered prudent and wise in this life if we save money in a bank for our retirement years. How much wiser is it to also store up treasure in heaven for the *next* life, a world where we'll spend all eternity!

6.

HEAVENLY REWARDS

THE TRUE TREASURE

Jesus admonished us to store up treasures in heaven, and the question arises: How *real* is this treasure? Is it merely a figurative way of saying we'll have joy and happiness there—or will this treasure also be something more tangible? While some of the Bible's descriptions of heaven may be symbolic, much is either literal or symbolizes a tangible reality. After the resurrection, our glorified bodies will be made of supernatural elements that will nevertheless be solid and material. So we'll be able to (and desire to) enjoy tangible possessions. We won't simply float in a cloud bank feeling joyful. Bear this in mind when considering Jesus' promise:

> *"Look, I am coming soon! My reward is*
> *with me, and I will give to each person*
> *according to what they have done."*
> REVELATION 22:12 NIV

Jesus repeatedly promised in the Bible that the good we do here will be rewarded in heaven:

> *For the Son of man shall come in the glory*
> *of his Father with his angels; and then*
> *he shall reward every man*
> *according to his works.*
> MATTHEW 16:27 KJV

So although we'll receive joy and peace in large measure in the hereafter, many of our rewards—the heavenly mansions, for example—will likely be tangible supernatural things.

RUNNING FOR THE ETERNAL PRIZE

The apostle Paul described this brief life as a race—and we are running toward the finish line. Unlike a standard Olympian race, we aren't competing against other people. We're simply trying to do our personal best. Paul compares an earthly race to our spiritual course:

> *Don't you realize that in a race everyone*
> *runs, but only one person gets the*
> *prize? So run to win! All athletes are*
> *disciplined in their training. They do it*
> *to win a prize that will fade away, but*
> *we do it for an eternal prize.*
> 1 CORINTHIANS 9:24–25 NLT

The prize we receive at the end of this race is eternal life in heaven. That is guaranteed to all those who finish the course here on earth. Paul also said:

> *Forgetting the past and looking forward*
> *to what lies ahead, I press on to reach the*

> *end of the race and receive the heavenly*
> *prize for which God, through Christ*
> *Jesus, is calling us.*
> PHILIPPIANS 3:13–14 NLT

THE JUDGMENT SEAT OF CHRIST

The Bible tells us also that we must one day appear before the judgment seat of Christ, to give an account of our lives—for both our words and our deeds. Jesus warned, "'But I say to you that for every idle word men may speak, they will give account of it in the day of judgment'" (Matthew 12:36 NKJV). The apostle Paul tells us:

> *Remember, we will all stand before the*
> *judgment seat of God. . . . Yes, each of us*
> *will give a personal account to God.*
> ROMANS 14:10, 12 NLT

We will be required to give an *account* of how we lived our lives on this earth. But then we will be *rewarded* in proportion to the good we have done—or suffer loss for the wrong we have done or the good we failed to do.

> *For we must all appear before the judgment*
> *seat of Christ, so that each of us may receive*
> *what is due us for the things done while in*
> *the body, whether good or bad.*
>
> 2 CORINTHIANS 5:10 NIV

The Greek word in these two verses translated as "judgment seat" is *bema*—and in the Greek Olympic Games the bema was *not* a tribunal that judged someone guilty or innocent and decided punishments. Rather, the bema was a place of awards. It was where the judges sat and gave crowns (laurel wreaths) to the winners of various events. Those who appeared before the judgment seat were those already recognized as having won the race.

This judgment is not to determine whether we go to heaven or to hell. Our eternal destination was decided the day we trusted Christ to save us. We will enter heaven because our names are already written in the Lamb's Book of Life.

This judgment is *not* the judgment of the unsaved that happens at the end of the Millennium (Revelation 20:11–15), where God determines the punishment of the unsaved. The judgment seat of Christ happens when we—the redeemed—appear before Him who saved us. This judgment will determine how we are rewarded. It will be a very loving and fair judgment—but it will be thorough. As Paul wrote:

> *For no other foundation can anyone lay than that which is laid, which is Jesus Christ. Now if anyone builds on this foundation with gold, silver, precious stones, wood, hay, straw, each one's work will become clear; for the Day will declare it, because it will be revealed by fire; and the fire will test each one's work, of what sort it is. If anyone's work which he has built on it endures, he will receive a reward. If anyone's work is burned, he will suffer loss; but he himself will be saved, yet so as through fire.*
>
> 1 CORINTHIANS 3: 11–15 NKJV

Even if we lived futile lives, doing little or nothing for Christ, our salvation remains secure. But what a terrible, needless loss to see the selfish ambition and self-seeking works of years burned away. Nevertheless, we are forgiven and will remain in Christ's love.

> *And because He loved me and forgave me, I am on the way to heaven, and I shall see His face and sing His praises. When I have sinned, He has loved me; when I have forgotten Him, He has loved me; and He will love me when my knees tremble and my hair is gray. He will bear and carry His servant; and He will love me forever and ever.*
> CHARLES SPURGEON

THE CROWN OF LIFE

This brings us to our next subject—the heavenly crowns God has promised to those who love Him. Meditate on the following promises.

Blessed is the man who endures
temptation; for. . .he will receive the
crown of life which the Lord has
promised to those who love Him.
JAMES 1:12 NKJV

"Be faithful until death, and I will
give you the crown of life."
REVELATION 2:10 NKJV

Some Christians envision these crowns as some kind of heavyset, spiked, medieval head-wear—but this is a misunderstanding of the Greek word *stephanos* translated as "crown" in the New Testament. Stephanos actually means "circlet" when it refers to a royal crown (Revelation 6:2). This circlet is, incidentally, more or less shaped like a halo, and may be the source of the popular concept of halos of light. But these crowns don't hover above the wearers' heads.

In the New Testament, though, stephanos usually refers not to circular crowns but to laurel wreaths. During the Greek Olympic Games of the apostle Paul's day, winners of races and other events were crowned with a wreath of laurel leaves—a garland—that the judge placed on their heads. Paul describes this as a "perishable crown."

> *And everyone who competes for the*
> *prize is temperate in all things. Now*
> *they do it to obtain a perishable crown,*
> *but we for an imperishable crown.*
> 1 CORINTHIANS 9:25 NKJV

The "crown of life" is also called the "crown of righteousness." It is given not just to the greatest saints, but to all true Christians.

> *And now the prize awaits me—the*
> *crown of righteousness, which the Lord,*
> *the righteous Judge, will give me on the*
> *day of his return. And the prize is not*
> *just for me but for all who eagerly look*
> *forward to his appearing.*
> 2 TIMOTHY 4:8 NLT

Very likely, the luster and glory of our crown will depend in large measure on how we live our lives for Christ here below.

Picture in your mind that moment when Jesus Christ will salute you as "more than a conqueror" and put a pearly crown upon your head more glittering than stars.

CHARLES SPURGEON

DIFFERENT KINDS OF CROWNS

Our crown will not only be imperishable, but far more glorious than the Greek athletes' quickly-fading laurel crowns. The apostle Peter tells us,

And when the Chief Shepherd appears, you will receive the crown of glory that will never fade away.

1 PETER 5:4 NIV

However—and here is an interesting point—some Bible scholars believe that when Peter talks about the "crown of glory," this is *separate* from the "crown of life." Can someone have more than one crown in heaven? Jesus does. Since He is the "King of kings" John describes Him as having *many* crowns on His head (Revelation 19:12).

In the verse above, Peter was talking to elders and shepherds (pastors) who watched over churches and set an example for believers. He said that if they served Christ well, they'd receive a crown of glory. The crown of life is given to *all* believers, and can't be lost—but the crown of glory is an award for exceptional service. It appears that people *can* lose this crown by not fulfilling what God has called them to do. Perhaps that is what the following verse refers to:

> *"Hold fast what you have,*
> *that no one may take your crown."*
> REVELATION 3:11 NKJV

If God has given you a job to do or a ministry to fulfill and you refuse, He will find others to do your job—and they will receive the reward.

Stars in Your Crown

The expression "stars in my crown" is more of a poetic picture than a scriptural doctrine—but there is something to the idea. The clearest representation of this was when John saw a vision of the Church, symbolized as a woman:

> *And there appeared a great wonder in*
> *heaven; a woman clothed with the sun,*
> *and the moon under her feet, and upon*
> *her head a crown of twelve stars.*
> Revelation 12:1 kjv

The twelve stars on her head symbolized either the twelve tribes of Israel or Jesus' twelve apostles. Yet in Christian hymns, "stars" often referred to rewards that Christ gives us—especially for winning souls to Him. This imagery comes from the book of Daniel:

"Those who are wise will shine like the brightness of the heavens, and those who lead many to righteousness, like the stars for ever and ever."

DANIEL 12:3 NIV

In addition, we have Paul's statements that the people he won to Christ were his "crown." Paul called the Christians of Philippi "my brethren dearly beloved and longed for, my joy and crown" (Philippians 4:1 KJV), and he asked the Christians of Thessalonica, "For what is our hope, or joy, or crown of rejoicing? Is it not even you?" (1 Thessalonians 2:19 NKJV).

Great preachers like Spurgeon wove these verses together to create the following word picture:

Oh, think of the crowns that are in heaven! So many souls, so many gems! Have you ever thought what it would be to wear in heaven a starless crown? All the saints will have crowns, but those who win souls will have a star in their crown for every soul. Some of you, my

> *friends, will wear a crown without a*
> *star; would you like that?*
>
> CHARLES SPURGEON

This thought is also embodied in the following hymn:

> *O what joy it will be when His face I*
>   *behold,*
> *Living gems at his feet to lay down!*
> *It would sweeten my bliss in the city of*
>   *gold,*
> *Should there be any stars in my crown.*

> REFRAIN
> *Will there be any stars, any stars in my*
>   *crown*
> *When at evening the sun goeth down?*
> *When I wake with the blest in the man-*
>   *sions of rest*
> *Will there be any stars in my crown?*

"WILL THERE BE ANY STARS IN MY CROWN?"
BY ELIZA E. HEWITT, C. 1897

Certainly we shall be rewarded for winning others to faith in Jesus, and some Christians believe that this reward will be a distinct soul-winner's crown. Others maintain we will receive a symbolic "star" in our crown of life for every soul we win. *Whatever* form our reward takes, the Lord will make sure that it is glorious!

GREAT REWARDS IN HEAVEN

Jesus assures us that we will be rewarded greatly for living wholeheartedly for Him. For example, those who suffer persecution because they stand up for Him will be recompensed beyond measure.

> *Blessed are ye, when men shall hate you,*
> *and when they shall separate you from*
> *their company, and shall reproach you,*
> *and cast out your name as evil, for the*
> *Son of man's sake. Rejoice ye in that*
> *day, and leap for joy: for, behold, your*
> *reward is great in heaven.*
> LUKE 6:22–23 KJV

If you've ever suffered for your faith in Christ, if you've ever been mocked or humiliated or tormented because you are a Christian, take comfort in the following promise:

> *For I consider that the sufferings of this present time are not worthy to be compared with the glory which shall be revealed in us.*
> ROMANS 8:18 NKJV

We will also be marvelously rewarded for obeying Christ's difficult commands. For example, He told us to love our enemies and to do good even to the unthankful and evil. That's how much love God has, and Jesus tells us *we* need that kind of love, as well. Difficult? Yes, certainly! But those who love greatly will be rewarded greatly.

> *But love ye your enemies, and do good, and lend, hoping for nothing again; and your reward shall be great, and ye shall be the children of the Highest: for he is kind unto the unthankful and to the evil.*
> LUKE 6:35 KJV

FACES GLOWING LIKE THE SUN

> *Life on earth is but a vapor,*
> *Soon we'll lay these bodies down;*
> *But if we continue faithful,*
> *We shall wear the victor's crown—*
>
> *Brighter than the stars of heaven,*
> *Brighter than the dazzling sun,*
> *We shall shine among the ransomed,*
> *When our work on earth is done.*

"SAINTS' REWARD"
BY WILLIAM G. SCHELL, PUBLISHED 1911

When He stood on a mountain with Peter, James, and John, "Jesus' appearance was transformed so that his face shone like the sun, and his clothes became as white as light" (Matthew 17:2 NLT). And when the apostle John saw Jesus years later in heaven in His glorified, resurrected body, he described Him this way:

> *The hair on his head was white like*
> *wool, as white as snow, and his eyes*

> were like blazing fire. His feet were
> like bronze glowing in a furnace, and
> his voice was like the sound of rushing
> waters. . . . His face was like the sun
> shining in all its brilliance.
> REVELATION 1:14–16 NIV

The same apostle tells us, "But we know that when Christ appears, we shall be like him, for we shall see him as he is" (1 John 3:2 NIV). The Lord's face shone like the sun, and so will ours—to a lesser degree, of course. Jesus himself said:

> Then shall the righteous shine forth as
> the sun in the kingdom of their Father.
> MATTHEW 13:43 KJV

This, by the way, is why—in classic art—plate-shaped discs often appear behind the heads of saints such as Moses. This disc represents a glow radiating from his face. After spending forty days and nights in the presence of God, the skin of Moses' face glowed with the glory of the Lord (Exodus 34:28–30). Many

Christians believe this same thing will happen to us when we get our resurrection bodies. Here on earth, in our physical bodies, we can be full of the Holy Spirit. In heaven, apparently God's Spirit within us will literally cause us to glow.

DIFFERENT LIKE THE STARS

Every star in the universe is different, and there are hints in the Bible that our new bodies will glow with varying amounts of spiritual radiance.

> *There is one glory of the sun, another*
> *glory of the moon, and another glory*
> *of the stars; for one star differs from*
> *another star in glory.*
> 1 CORINTHIANS 15:41 NKJV

Perhaps this is part of our eternal reward. The closer we are to God on earth—the more we treasure spending time in His presence—the more some of His glory will be imparted to us. Of course, our heavenly rewards won't be determined just by the quality of our time spent in prayer, but how we live our lives after we rise from prayer.

For as one star another far exceeds,
So souls in heaven are placed by their deeds.
ROBERT GREENE

THE RAPTURE AND RESURRECTION

When we die, our spirit leaves our body and goes directly to heaven. As long as we exist in that state, we're a spirit without a body. But God doesn't intend for us to be this way forever. Just as He resurrected His Son Jesus from the dead, He will also raise up our physical bodies as well.

But if the Spirit of Him who raised Jesus
from the dead dwells in you, He who
raised Christ from the dead will also
give life to your mortal bodies through
His Spirit who dwells in you.
ROMANS 8:11 NKJV

Some people mistakenly think that we receive our resurrection bodies the instant we go to heaven—but this isn't the case. The resurrection from the dead happens on the day of Christ's second coming, which is still a future event. Those who have died will return with Christ at that time, and their bodies will rise as glorified supernatural bodies to reunite with their spirits. Then those of us who are living will be transformed where we stand and will be caught up into the air to join Jesus and the other saints:

> *For the Lord himself shall descend from*
> *heaven with a shout, with the voice of the*
> *archangel, and with the trump of God:*
> *and the dead in Christ shall rise first:*
> *Then we which are alive and remain shall*
> *be caught up together with them in the*
> *clouds, to meet the Lord in the air.*
> 1 THESSALONIANS 4:16–17 KJV

Living or deceased, we shall all be changed in an instant and become *truly* living.

> *We shall not all sleep, but we shall all be*
> *changed—in a moment, in the*
> *twinkling of an eye, at the last trumpet.*
> *For the trumpet will sound,*
> *and the dead will be raised incorruptble,*
> *and we shall be changed.*
>
> 1 CORINTHIANS 15:51–52 NKJV

OUR RESURRECTION BODY

We will definitely be changed, but what exactly will our resurrected bodies be like? Though they're natural physical bodies now—perishable and weak—they will become glorious, powerful, eternal bodies:

> *So also is the resurrection of the dead.*
> *The body is sown in corruption, it is*
> *raised in incorruption. It is sown in*
> *dishonor, it is raised in glory. It is sown*
> *in weakness, it is raised in power.*
> *It is sown a natural body, it is raised*
> *a spiritual body.*
>
> 1 CORINTHIANS 15:42–44 NKJV

When our bodies are transformed in that day, we will be very much like Jesus.

> *Look up to Jesus now, let the eye of your*
> *faith behold Him with many crowns*
> *upon His head, and remember that you*
> *will one day be like Him, when you shall*
> *see Him as He is; you shall not be so*
> *great as He is, you shall not be so divine,*
> *but still you shall, in a measure, share*
> *the same honors and enjoy the same*
> *happiness and the same dignity*
> *which He possesses.*
>
> CHARLES SPURGEON

THE MARRIAGE SUPPER OF THE LAMB

There will be a great feast in heaven one day, when we've all arrived there. This feast is called the Marriage Supper of the Lamb. All genuine Christians will be present at this gathering, and we will be truly blessed to be there.

Blessed are they which are called unto
the marriage supper of the Lamb.
REVELATION 19:9 KJV

As Paul tells us, the Church—the entire body of believers worldwide—is the Bride of Christ. Right now we are "betrothed" to Christ. That is, we are engaged to be married.

For I have betrothed you to one husband,
that I may present you as a
chaste virgin to Christ.
2 CORINTHIANS 11:2 NKJV

One day, a wedding will happen in heaven.

"Let us be glad and rejoice and give Him
glory, for the marriage of the Lamb has
come, and His wife has made herself
ready." And to her it was granted to be
arrayed in fine linen, clean and bright.
REVELATION 19:7–8 NKJV

That this marriage is symbolic of a spiritual union is obvious. In the very same book of Revelation, John also describes the celestial city, the new Jerusalem, as the Bride of Christ:

> *Then I, John, saw the holy city,*
> *New Jerusalem, coming down*
> *out of heaven from God,*
> *prepared as a bride adorned*
> *for her husband.*
> REVELATION 21:2 NKJV

> *Then one of the seven angels. . .*
> *came and said to me, "Come with me!*
> *I will show you the bride,*
> *the wife of the Lamb."*
> *So he. . .showed me the*
> *holy city, Jerusalem,*
> *descending out of heaven from God.*
> REVELATION 21:9–10 NLT

God compares us to these eternal heavenly abodes—His city, His temple—because, just as He dwells in these places, so He dwells in our hearts.

For you are the temple of the living God.
As God has said: "I will dwell in them
and walk among them. I will be their
God, and they shall be My people."

2 CORINTHIANS 6:16 NKJV

Not all the music blown from sweet
instruments or drawn from living strings
can yield such melody as this sweet
promise "I will be their God." Here is
a deep sea of bliss, a shoreless ocean of
delight; come, bathe your spirit in it;
swim, and you will find no shore; dive
throughout eternity, and you will find
no bottom. "I will be their God."

CHARLES SPURGEON

RULING AND REIGNING ON EARTH

For many Christians, the following scripture is one of the more fascinating promises that Christ makes to us as believers:

*Blessed and holy are those who share in
the first resurrection. The second death
has no power over them, but they will
be priests of God and of Christ and will
reign with Him for a thousand years.*
REVELATION 20:6 NIV

The Bible tells us that "the first resurrection," the resurrection of the saved, happens when Christ returns to earth. This is followed by the great Battle of Armageddon, when the nations of the earth are gathered together to wage war against Jesus Christ. After defeating their armies, Jesus will reign over the surviving people of the earth. And He says that we will reign *with* him:

*"To all who are victorious, who obey
me to the very end, to them I will give
authority over all the nations. They will
rule the nations with an iron rod."*
REVELATION 2:26–27 NLT

We will not only rule as kings and queens over the nations of this world, but will act as priests, teaching the inhabitants of the earth about God:

> *"[You] have made us kings and priests to our God; and we shall reign on the earth."*
> REVELATION 5:10 NKJV

Obviously, there will be millions upon millions of Christians in heaven at that day, and the nations of the world don't need *that* many rulers. So it's likely that the more faithful and capable Christians will be leaders at a national level. Under them others will rule over states and provinces and districts. And beneath them, still others will govern individual cities and towns. However we personally reign on the earth, it will be an exciting time.

7.

HEAVEN ON EARTH

THE NEW JERUSALEM ON EARTH

Right now, the home of God—the heavenly city, the new Jerusalem—is in the spiritual dimension. Paul called it "the Jerusalem above" (Galatians 4:26 NKJV). But after the end of the thousand-year Millennium, God will dissolve this present earth and burn its atmosphere (2 Peter 3:10). Then He will renew our planet and give it a new "heaven" (or atmosphere).

> *Then I saw a new heaven and a new*
> *earth, for the old heaven and the old*
> *earth had disappeared. And the sea*
> *was also gone.*
> REVELATION 21:1 NLT

When this world has been renewed and its entire surface transformed into a paradise, God's city will emerge from the heavenly dimension and descend to earth:

> *I saw the Holy City, the new Jerusalem,*
> *coming down out of heaven from God. . . .*
> *And I heard a loud voice from the throne*
> *saying, "Look! God's dwelling place is*
> *now among the people, and he will*
> *dwell with them."*
> REVELATION 21:2–3 NIV

Not only will the heavenly city be on earth, but the entire planet will be an absolute Garden of Eden. It will truly be heaven on earth.

> *O the transporting, rapturous scene,*
> *That rises to my sight!*

Sweet fields arrayed in living green,
And rivers of delight!

REFRAIN
There generous fruits that never fail,
On trees immortal grow;
There rocks and hills, and brooks and
* vales,*
With milk and honey flow.

Over all those wide extended plains
Shines one eternal day;
There God the Son forever reigns,
And scatters night away.

"ON JORDAN'S STORMY BANKS I STAND"
BY SAMUEL STENNETT, BEFORE 1795

THE HEAVENLY CITY

The following passages—from the final, climactic chapters of Revelation—describe what the heavenly city is like:

Her light was like a most precious stone,
like a jasper stone, clear as crystal.
Also she had a great and high wall
with twelve gates, and twelve angels at
the gates, and names written on them,
which are the names of the twelve tribes
of the children of Israel: three gates on
the east, three gates on the north,
three gates on the south,
and three gates on the west.
REVELATION 21:11–13 NKJV

Christians have differing opinions whether these descriptions of the heavenly city are meant to be taken literally or symbolically. But if the mansions within the city are literal and the streets of gold are of solid material, surely the city itself is tangible. If it's different from what we read in Revelation that will be because it's so much better that John's words fell short of describing its full beauty and wonder.

The construction of its wall was of jasper;
and the city was pure gold, like clear glass.
The foundations of the wall of the city

> *were adorned with all kinds of precious*
> *stones. . . . The twelve gates were twelve*
> *pearls: each individual gate was of one*
> *pearl. And the street of the city was pure*
> *gold, like transparent glass.*
> REVELATION 21:18–19, 21 NKJV

Are the gates of the city actual pearls? More likely they're gigantic orbs glowing with pearl-like luster. After all, they weren't fashioned like ordinary pearls nor are they, in fact, made of natural, terrestrial elements at all.

> *But I saw no temple in it, for the Lord*
> *God Almighty and the Lamb are its*
> *temple. The city had no need of the sun*
> *or of the moon to shine in it,*
> *for the glory of God illuminated it.*
> *The Lamb is its light.*
> REVELATION 21:22–23 NKJV

As you recall from an earlier chapter, whenever the heavens opened and God appeared to men, they saw that He was glowing with great light. This light is called the "glory of

145

the Lord," and it fills and illuminates the entire city.

A Lakeside, Woodland Heaven

One passage offers a fascinating look into what heaven will be like on the *rest* of the globe. While describing the heavenly city, John said:

> *And the nations of those who are saved*
> *shall walk in its light, and the kings of*
> *the earth bring their glory and honor*
> *into it. Its gates shall not be shut at all*
> *by day (there shall be no night there).*
> *And they shall bring the glory and the*
> *honor of the nations into it.*
> Revelation 21:24–26 nkjv

Great Bible commentators of the past have marveled at this amazing description.

The heavenly state is described as a
paradise, a paradise in a city or a whole
city in paradise. In the first paradise

there were only two persons to behold
the beauty of it, but in this second
paradise whole cities and nations shall
find abundant delight and satisfaction.
MATTHEW HENRY

This also brings up intriguing questions: If the saved live *inside* the heavenly city, then who are these saved people living *outside*, who bring the best of their produce and goods into the city? They're obviously redeemed believers, too, so what are they doing outside the city? There's a plausible explanation that fulfills many people's fondest dreams.

Many people, while they're enthralled by descriptions of a shining city of transparent gold, *also* long to be surrounded by the beauty of nature. They'll be thankful for a mansion inside the heavenly Jerusalem, and walk streets lined by the trees of life, but they long for a country house surrounded by peaceful nature—lakes and streams, meadows and woodland glades filled with deer and birds and other peaceful creatures. They dream of a bit of acreage with a cottage where they can putter in a garden, walk their dog, chat leisurely, even fish.

Is this too much to ask, or is it out of the question?

It seems that such people are going to get their wish. They will enjoy the best of both worlds—life in the transcendently beautiful city of God, *and* life in the Eden-like tranquil countryside outside the city. And apparently they'll be growing fruit and other food which they'll then bring into the city. Even though we'll be immortal, we'll still eat food—so someone will need to grow it. While this is admittedly speculation, the scripture seems to indicate that it could be the case.

Also, the fact that there are still "kings" over the nations of the world shows that we'll still rule and reign with Christ after the Millennium. The Bible indicates that we'll serve God for eternity (Revelation 22:3), and "serving" means *doing* something. In fact, the Bible says, "And they shall reign forever and ever" (Revelation 22:5 NKJV). What will we reign over?

Here we explore *other* people's dreams and wishes, and seek to answer the question: "What will we do for all eternity?"

Beyond Heaven on Earth

We will have forever and ever to worship God, ask Him questions, learn whatever we wish to learn, talk with fascinating saints of God from ages past, relax, and so on. During this entire time, the Bible tells us we'll continue to serve God. We'll continue to reign with him, world without end. But surely, many people reason— even after we do every conceivable thing we could imagine doing on this earth—the day will come when we'll look for *new* horizons, *new* worlds to explore.

Here is where many Christians let their imaginations run wild with exciting possibilities. When they think of "new worlds to explore," they don't think of them in a figurative sense. They think of new worlds *literally*. Why not? When God created our sun, "he made the stars also" (Genesis 1:16 KJV). Now, astronomers estimate that there are two hundred billion to four hundred billion stars just in our Milky Way Galaxy alone. And they guess that there are some 170 billion galaxies in the universe. You do the math: that's a *lot* of stars!

How astonishingly creative God is!

Recently, scientists have discovered something that they've suspected all along—that our sun is not the only star with planets. They have detected hundreds of planets orbiting nearby stars, and they calculate that our galaxy has some 50 billion planets, of which 500 million are within the habitable zone of their star. Think of that! Some 500 million planets in our galaxy alone can potentially support life! There's obviously no need to worry that we'll run out of things to do and see and rule over in eternity.

Some Christians note that God created habitable planets like Earth for the express purpose of being inhabited (Isaiah 45:18). But whether life exists elsewhere or not, whether alien worlds are teeming with exotic flora and fauna, we simply can't say. Christian scholars like C.S. Lewis believed this was possible. Although this is a fascinating topic, it's entirely beyond the scope of this book. If any such thing *does* exist, remember that it was God (through Christ) who created it:

All things were made through Him,
and without Him nothing was made
that was made.
JOHN 1:3 NKJV

Our future is definitely not going to be boring! We'll have all of eternity to explore heaven and the vastness of God's Creation.

UNTIL THAT DAY

Until then, we're still on earth doing our best to follow Jesus' commandments. It's not always an easy road we walk—but one day soon we'll experience what God has prepared for us, and we'll realize that it has been worth it all.

As surely as you are God's child today,
so surely shall all your trials soon be
at an end, and you shall be rich to all
the intents of bliss. Wait awhile, and
that weary head shall wear the crown
of glory; and that hand of labor shall
grasp the palm branch of victory. Do not

lament your troubles, but rather rejoice
that before long you will be where "there
shall be neither sorrow nor crying,
neither shall there be any more pain."
The everlasting song is almost on
your lips. The portals of heaven
stand open for you.
CHARLES SPURGEON

SCRIPTURE INDEX